playful & sassy
Lariat Necklaces

Red Lariat Necklace

MATERIALS: 14 AB-Crystal 6mm cube beads • 12 AB-Siam 8mm faceted beads • 54 Siam 6mm bicone beads • 26 AB-Crystal 4mm bicone beads • 90 Siam 4mm faceted beads • 48" of Clear elastic cord

INSTRUCTIONS:

Slip on beads as shown in beading diagram. Repeat to make 11 sets. Slip both cords through 6mm bicone, cube and 6mm bicone. Next, slip beads on one cord following tassel diagram. Tie knot by slipping cord around last 4mm bead and through 6mm bead before tying around cord. Repeat on other side.

Necklace

Necklace Tassel

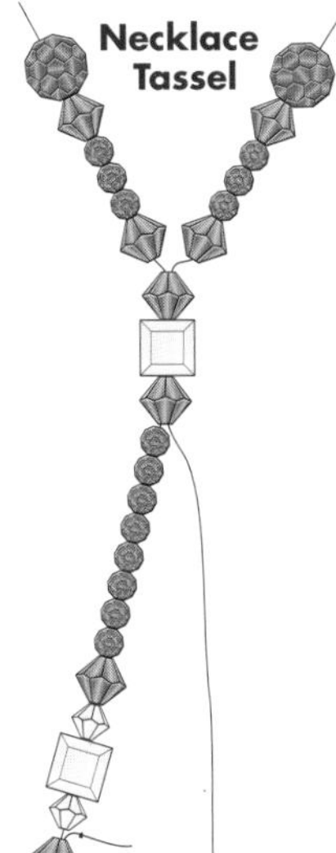

36" Blue Lariat Necklace

MATERIALS: 264 Sapphire 4mm bicone beads • 32 Sapphire 6mm bicone beads • 64 Sterling Silver 3mm beads • 2 yards of Clear elastic cord

INSTRUCTIONS: Cut 48" of cord. Slip 23 sets of beads on cord following necklace diagram. Do not trim excess cord, it will be used to tie on the tassels.

Tassels - Cut four 6" lengths of cord, slip beads for tassel on one 6" cord. Tie each end of cord in a knot by slipping cord around 3mm Silver bead and through 6mm bicone bead. Tie double knot. Stretch cord slightly between knots. Repeat 3 times to complete 4 pieces for tassels. Tie tassel on necklace using extra cord extending from necklace. Wrap cord between center 2 beads of tassel pieces, around 3mm Silver bead and through 6mm bicone. Tie a double knot around cord. Repeat on other side of necklace.

Note: To wear Lariat Necklace, wrap necklace around neck and loop one end over other end one time as if tying a knot.

Necklace

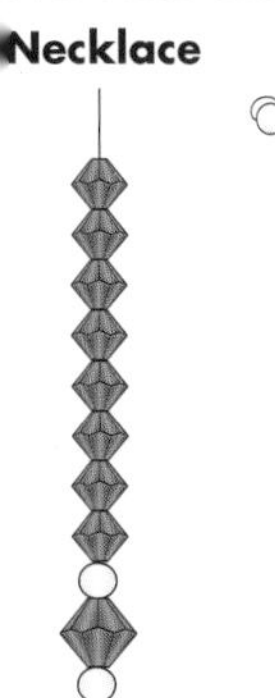

String Beads for Tassel

Attach Tassel

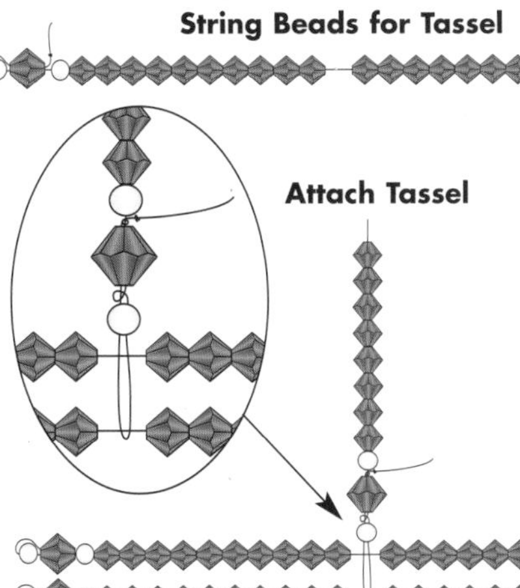

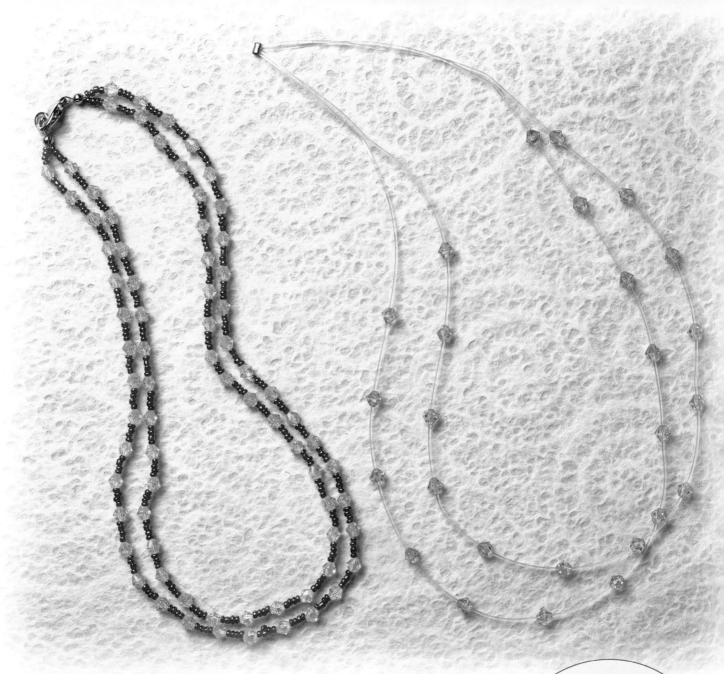

create your own

Crystal Necklace

BY DEBORAH CAMPBELL

Aqua Double Strand Necklace

MATERIALS: 76 Aqua 4mm bicone beads • Iridescent Blue seed beads • Beading thread and needle • 2 Silver clam shell bead tips • Silver lobster claw clasp • Silver jump ring

INSTRUCTIONS:

String 15½" and 17" strands of beads alternating 4 seed beads with bicone beads. On each end, pass threads through clam shell, seed bead, tie knot, trim ends and close shell. Attach clasp and jumpring to clam shells.

Illusion Necklace

MATERIALS: 26 Light Blue 6mm beads • Two 20" lengths of Clear elastic cord • Silver crimp bead • Glue

INSTRUCTIONS:

Beginning at center of cords, string and glue beads as shown. Pass ends of cord through crimp bead, flatten crimp and trim ends.

Clam Shell Bead Tip

Pass ends of cord through clam shell, seed bead, tie knot, trim ends and close shell.

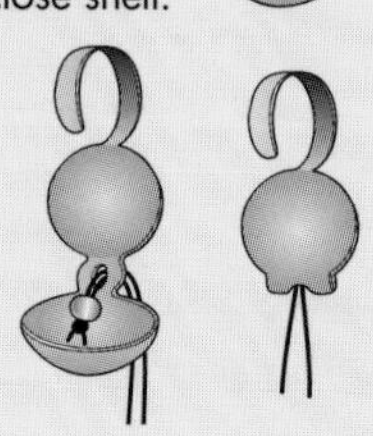

perfect balance

Jewelry Sets

Rondel Bracelet

MATERIALS: 11 Silver 6mm Crystal rondel beads • 22 6mm AB-Crystal spacer beads • 22 AB-Crystal 4mm bicone beads • 12" of Clear elastic cord

Rondel Earrings

MATERIALS: 2 Sterling Silver 4mm beads • 4 AB-Crystal 6mm spacer beads • 2 Silver Crystal 6mm rondel beads • 2 AB-Crystal 6mm faceted beads • 4 Sterling Silver head pins • 2 Sterling Silver french wires INSTRUCTIONS: For each earring, slip a 6mm AB faceted bead on head pin, trim pin ¼" above bead, make loop using round nose pliers. Trim head off another head pin, make a loop at one end. Slip on beads as shown. Trim pin, make a loop on other end. Connect loops from each set. Attach top loop to ear wire.

Rainbow Bracelet

MATERIALS: 10 multi color 6mm bicone beads • 20 Crystal 4mm bicone beads • 20 Sterling Silver 3mm beads • 12" of Clear elastic cord

Rainbow Earrings

MATERIALS: 16 Sterling Silver 3mm beads • 6 multi color 4mm bicone beads • 6" of Sterling Silver 24 gauge wire • 2 French ear wires. INSTRUCTIONS: For each earring, cut 3" of wire. Slip on beads as shown. Form beads into circle using pencil, twist wire to hold shape. Form loop in one wire with round nose pliers. Wrap that same wire around twisted area to secure loop. Trim off excess wire. Attach beads to ear wire by opening loop on ear wire.

Blue Bracelet

MATERIALS: 18 Aqua 6mm faceted beads • 18 Crystal 4mm faceted beads • 12" of Clear elastic cord

Heart Earrings

MATERIALS: 4 AB-Crystal 4mm faceted beads • 2 Aqua 6mm faceted beads • 2 Aqua 10mm hearts • 2 Gold filled 1" head pins • 2 Gold filled 5.8mm jump rings • 2 Gold filled ear posts with loop • 2 ear post clutches INSTRUCTIONS: For each earring, cut head off head pin, make loop. Slip beads on pin as shown, make a loop. Open jumpring, attach to heart and beaded pin. Close jumpring. Attach other end to ear post.

Cube Bracelet

BRACELET MATERIALS: 9 AB-Crystal 6mm cube beads • 9 AB-Crystal 4mm bicone beads • 36 Sterling Silver 3mm beads • 12" of Clear elastic cord

Cube Earring

MATERIALS: 6 Sterling Silver 3mm beads • 4 AB-Crystal 6mm cube beads • 2 Sterling Silver head pins • 2 Sterling Silver French ear wires INSTRUCTIONS: For each earring, slip beads on head pin as shown. Trim pin ¼" above beads, make loop using round nose pliers. Open loop slightly, slip on ear wire before closing.

Black & Crystal Bracelet

MATERIALS: 8 AB-Crystal 6mm faceted beads • 24 Black 4mm faceted beads • 16 Sterling Silver 3mm beads • 12" of Clear elastic cord

Black & Crystal Earrings

MATERIALS: 4 Sterling Silver 3mm beads • 2 Black 8mm faceted beads • 2 AB-Crystal 6mm faceted • 4 Sterling Silver 1" head pins • 2 Sterling Silver ear wires INSTRUCTIONS: For each earring, slip 6mm AB-faceted bead on head pin. Trim pin ¼" above beads, make a loop using round nose pliers. Trim head off another head pin, make loop at one end. Slip on beads as shown. Trim pin, make loop at other end. Connect loops from each set. Attach top loop to ear wire.

How To:

See Head Pin Dangle Instructions on page 9

ribbon & Crystals

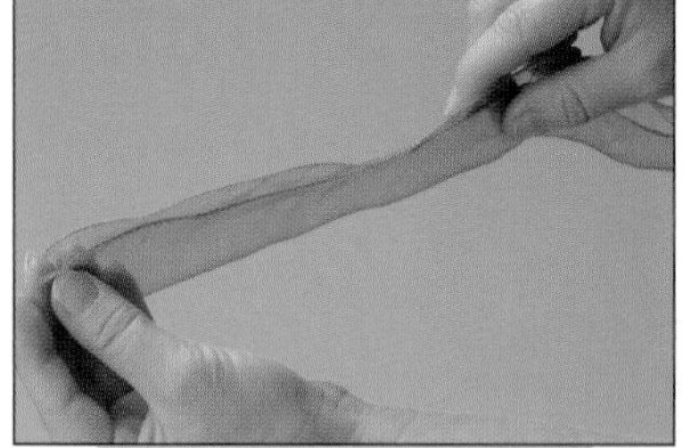

1. Fold ribbon in half lengthwise matching wire edges.

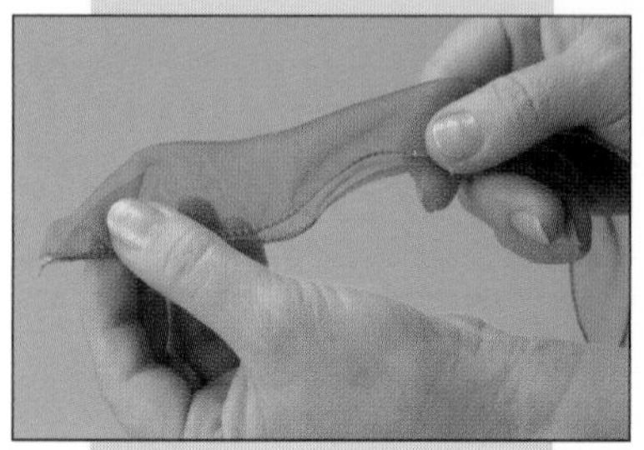

2. Fold the end down diagonally to bottom edge.

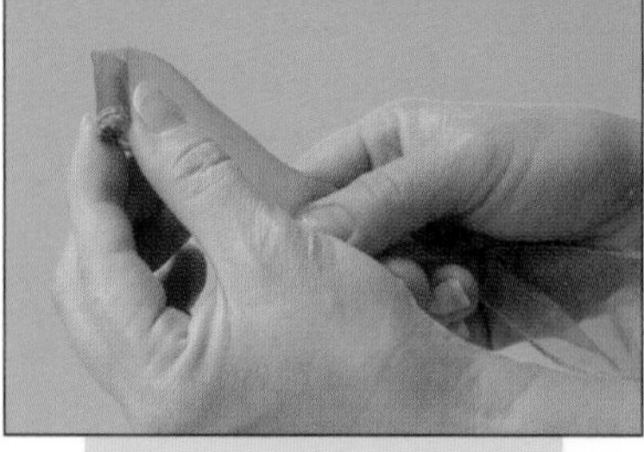

3. Roll ribbon around a pencil.

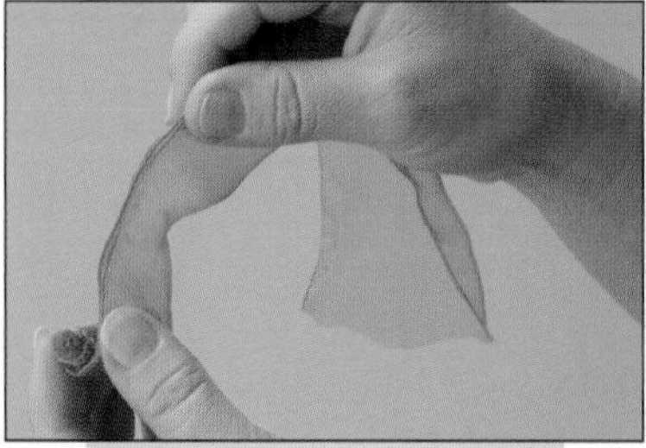

4. Continue rolling ribbon to form rosebud.

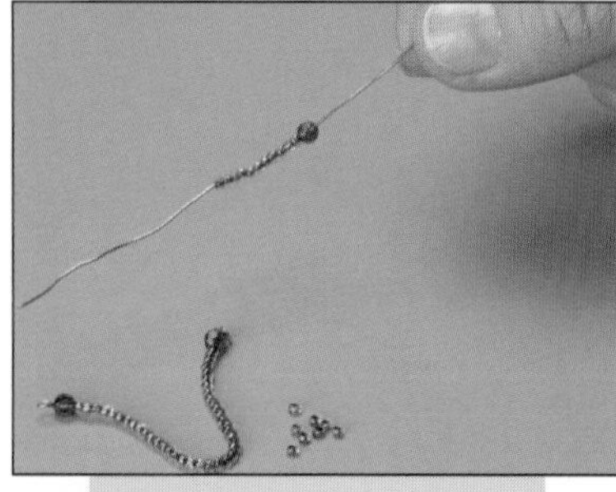

5. Thread the beads on the wire for accents

Crystal beads and luxurious ribbons come together here to give you a winning combination of style and romance.

Large Ribbon Rose Pin

MATERIALS: 2 Rose 6mm faceted beads • 4 Crystal 6mm bicone beads • Clear seed beads • 30" of 2½" Rose wire edge ribbon • Two 4" lengths of 2½" Green wire edge ribbon • 10" of Silver 26 gauge wire • Pin back • Needle and thread

INSTRUCTIONS:

1. Fold corner down on one edge of Rose ribbon. Begin rolling and folding ribbon to form rose. Sew to anchor in place as you roll.
2. String approximately 20 seed beads on wire, add one Crystal, one Light Rose, one Crystal. Add 20 seed beads. Twist ends of wire together forming circle. With one end, repeat beading sequence. Twist into circle.
3. Fold ends down on Green ribbon and shape into leaves. Attach beaded wire circles to leaves with free ends of wire. Sew leaves on back of rose.
4. Sew on pin back. Reshape rose and leaves.

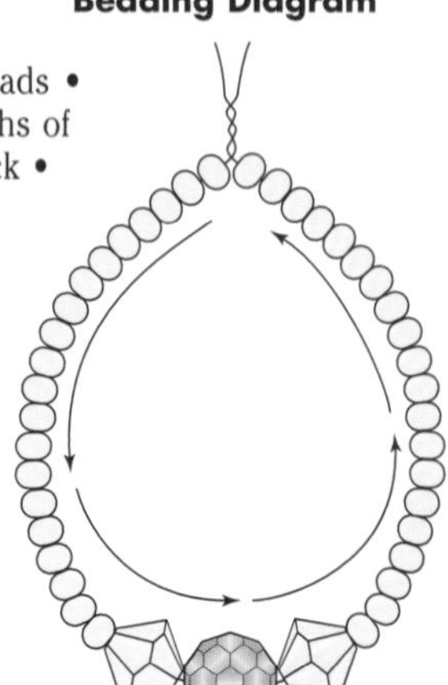

Rosebuds Pin

MATERIALS: 5 Amethyst 4mm faceted beads • 4 Amethyst 6mm faceted beads • 2 Amethyst 10mm hearts • Purple lined iridescent seed beads • 15", 10" and 8" lengths of 2½" Purple wire edge ribbon • Three 3" lengths of 2½" Green wire edge ribbon • 8" of Silver 26 gauge wire • Needle and thread

INSTRUCTIONS:

1. Fold Purple ribbon pieces in half lengthwise. Roll pieces into rosebuds. Fold Green ribbon pieces in half lengthwise, fold into leaves. Sew the buds and leaves together referring to photo for placement.
2. Form stamens with wire and beads. Slip base of stamens behind large bud. Sew in place.
3. Sew on pin back. Following diagram, sew dangles on bottom of rose, spacing evenly.

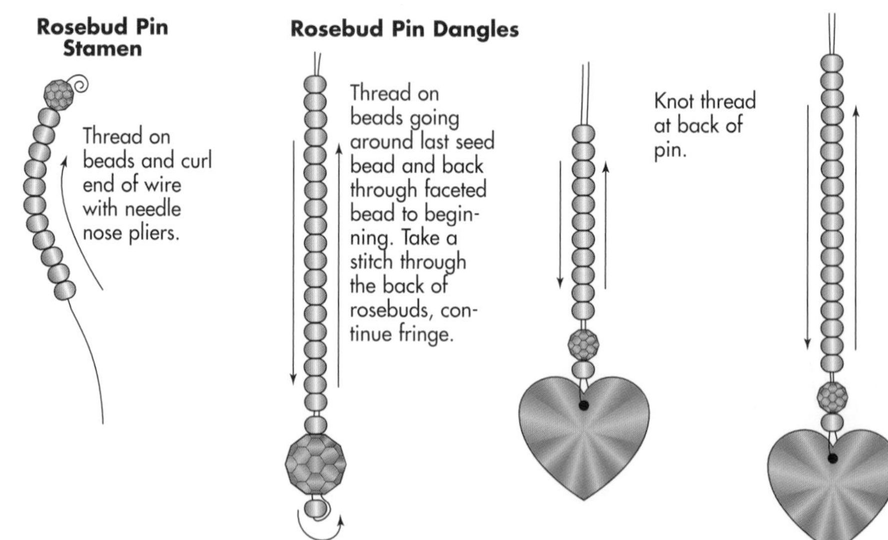

Rosebud Pin Stamen
Thread on beads and curl end of wire with needle nose pliers.
Rosebud Pin Dangles
Thread on beads going around last seed bead and back through faceted bead to beginning. Take a stitch through the back of rosebuds, continue fringe.
Knot thread at back of pin.

Ribbon Fan Pin

MATERIALS: 8 Topaz 4mm faceted beads • 2 Topaz 6mm faceted beads • 8mm Topaz faceted bead • 8" of 2½" Gold print wire edge ribbon • 8" of Gold 24 gauge wire • Pin back • Needle and thread • Craft glue

INSTRUCTIONS:

1. Fold over ¼" hem in end of ribbon, glue in place and let dry.
2. Fold fan into ¼" folds. Fold and glue hem in other end.
3. Make crystal ornament following diagram. Wrap around fan with free ends of wire.
4. Sew on pin back.

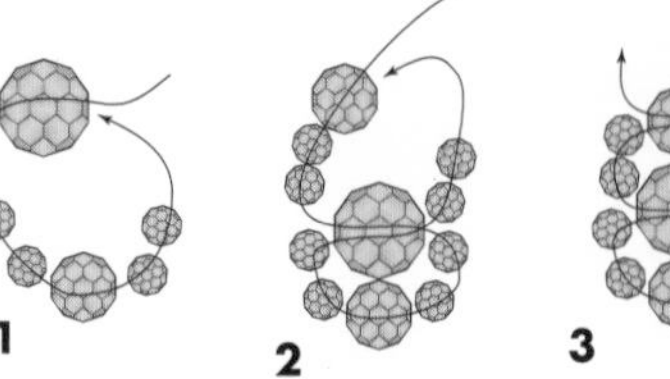

multiple personalities

Ribbon & Crystals

BY JANIE RAY

1. Glue hem in one end of the ribbon.

2. Fold the ribbon accordion style.

3. Sew the fold together on the back of fan.

4. Thread beads on the wire for bead ornament.

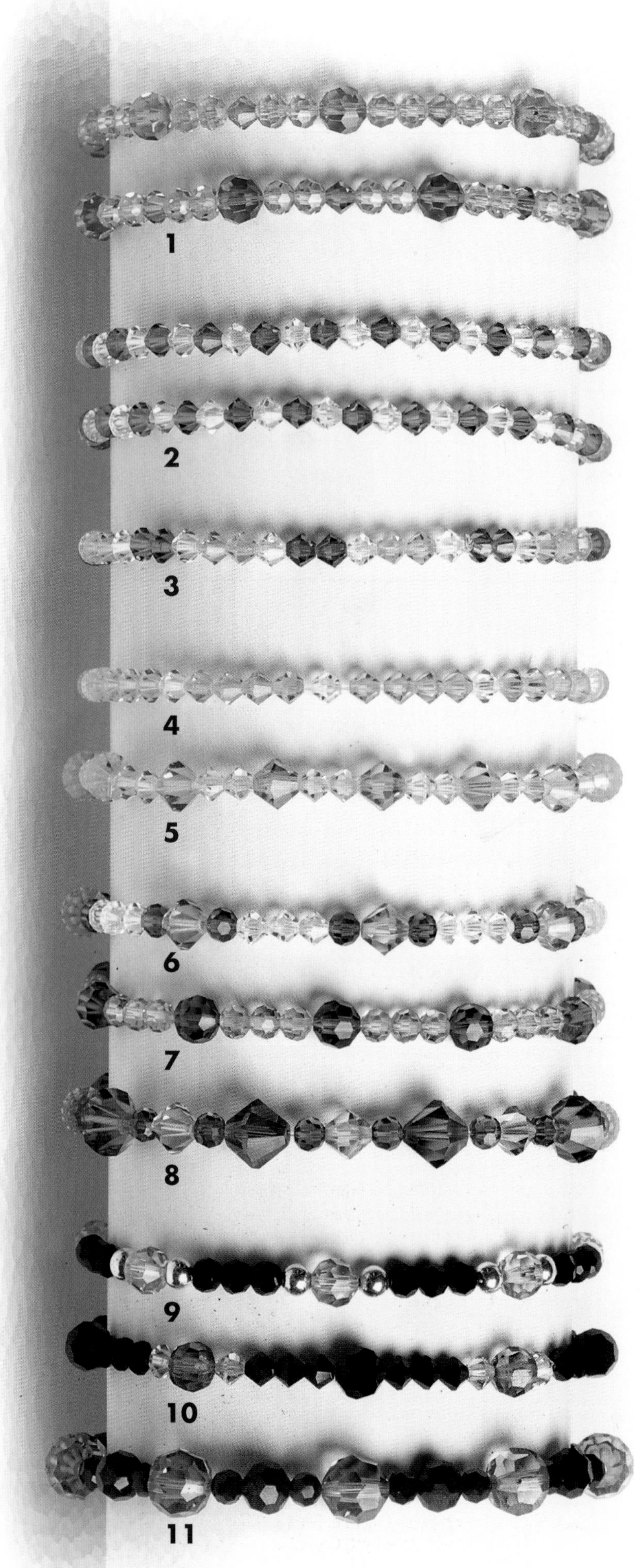

brilliant & beautiful

Basic Bracelets

Mix or match and make them your own. These Crystal beauties exude elegance as they glimmer and shimmer on your arm. Have a little fast fun!

The Basics

For a 7" bracelet, cut 12" of elastic cord. String beads as shown in photo. Tie a double knot and stretch the cord between knots. Trim the excess cord.

Bracelet 1

MATERIALS: 7 Sapphire 6mm faceted beads • 7 Sapphire 4mm bicone beads • 28 Aqua 4mm faceted beads • 12" of Clear elastic cord

Bracelet 2

MATERIALS: 24 Blue Zircon 4mm bicone beads • 24 Crystal 4mm bicone beads • 12" of Clear elastic cord

Bracelet 3

MATERIALS: 16 Blue Zircon 4mm bicone beads • 16 Rose 4mm bicone beads • 16 Crystal bicone beads • 12" of Clear elastic cord

Bracelet 4

MATERIALS: 36 Rose 4mm bicone beads • 9 Crystal 4mm bicone beads • 12" of Clear elastic cord

Bracelet 5

MATERIALS: 28 Light Rose 4mm bicone beads • 14 Rose 6mm bicone beads • 12" of Clear elastic cord

Bracelet 6

MATERIALS: 7 Light Amethyst 6mm bicone beads • 14 Amethyst 4mm faceted beads • 21 Crystal 4mm bicone beads • 12" of Clear elastic cord

Bracelet 7

MATERIALS: 10 Amethyst 6mm faceted beads • 30 Light Amethyst 4mm faceted beads • 12" of Clear elastic cord

Bracelet 8

MATERIALS: 8 Amethyst 8mm bicone beads • 8 Light Amethyst 6mm bicone beads • 16 Amethyst 4mm faceted beads • 12" of Clear elastic cord

Bracelet 9

MATERIALS: 7 Light Amethyst 6mm faceted beads • 21 Jet 4mm faceted beads • 14 Sterling Silver 4mm beads • 12" of Clear elastic cord

Bracelet 10

MATERIALS: 4 Black Diamond 6mm faceted beads • 4 Jet 6mm faceted beads • 24 Jet 4mm bicone beads • 8 Light Amethyst 4mm bicone beads • 12" of Clear elastic cord

Bracelet 11

MATERIALS: 8 Black Diamond 8mm faceted beads • 8 Jet 6mm faceted beads • 16 Jet 4mm faceted beads • 12" of Clear elastic cord

radiant rainbows

Bracelets & Earrings

BY DEBORAH CAMPBELL

Red Earrings

MATERIALS: 2 Siam 8mm faceted beads • 2 Siam 6mm faceted beads • 4 Sterling Silver 4mm beads • 2 Silver 1½" head pins • 2 Silver ear wires

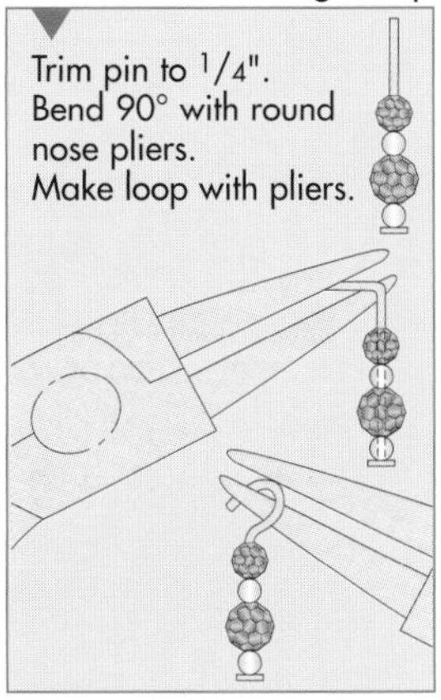

Daisy Bracelet

MATERIALS: 4 each of Jet, Sapphire, Aqua, Peridot, Emerald, Topaz, Siam, Rose, Light Rose, Light Amethyst, Amethyst and Black Diamond 4mm faceted beads • 12 Crystal 4mm faceted beads • 48" of Clear elastic cord
INSTRUCTIONS:
String beads following beading diagrams. Tie off as shown.

Head Pin Dangle Tip

Trim pin to 1/4".
Bend 90° with round nose pliers.
Make loop with pliers.

Daisy Beading Diagrams

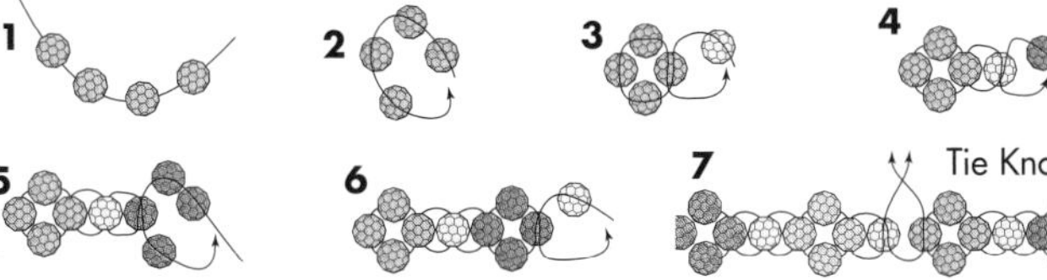

Circle Bracelet

MATERIALS: 8 Light Amethyst 8mm faceted beads • 8 Black Diamond 8mm faceted beads • 4 Siam 8mm faceted beads • 4 Tourmaline 6mm faceted beads • 8/0 Tourmaline seed beads • 2 Silver clam shell bead tips • 2 Silver 4mm jump rings • Silver toggle clasp • Beading thread and needles
INSTRUCTIONS:
Pass two 10" strands of thread through clam shell, tie knot, trim ends and close. String beads following beading diagrams. Add clam shell. Attach clasp to clam shell with jump rings.

Circle Beading Diagrams

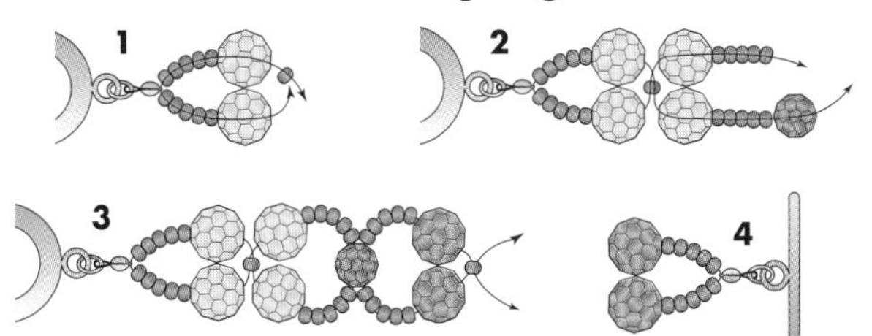

Rainbow Bracelet

MATERIALS: 2 each of Jet, Emerald, Peridot, Aqua, Sapphire, Garnet, Siam, Rose, Light Amethyst, Amethyst, Crystal and Black Diamond 8mm faceted beads • 12" of Clear elastic cord

How To:
See Head Pin Dangle Instructions on page 9

crystal & gold Bracelets & Earrings

BY DEBORAH CAMPBELL

Gold Loop Bracelet

BRACELET MATERIALS: 7 AB-Crystal 6mm faceted beads • 14 Gold filled 4mm beads • 70 Gold filled 3mm beads • 24" of Clear elastic cord
See instructions for Rose & Crystal Bracelet and use diagram below.

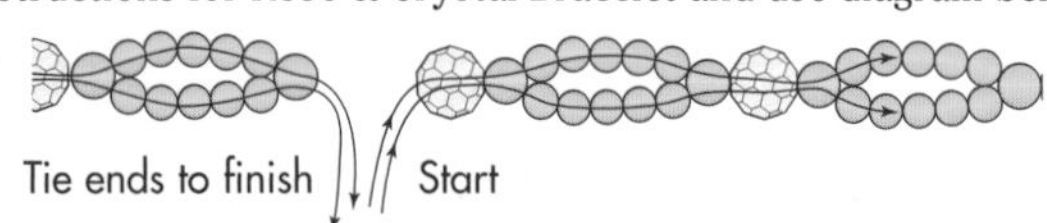

Gold Loop Earrings

MATERIALS: 8 AB-Crystal 4mm faceted beads • 4 AB-Crystal 6mm faceted beads • 8 Gold filled 3mm beads • 2 AB-Crystal 11.5mm x 5mm teardrop beads • 12" of Gold filled 24 gauge wire • 2 ear wires
INSTRUCTIONS: For each earring, cut 6" of wire. Center teardrop on wire. Slip beads on wire as shown and twist wires to form beaded loop. Cut off one wire. Make loop with round nose pliers and wrap excess wire around previous twists. Trim end.

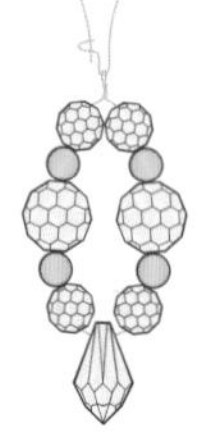
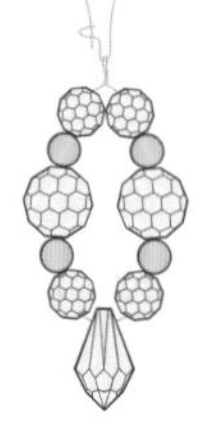
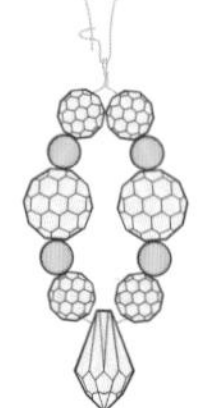

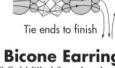

Rose & Crystal Earrings

MATERIALS: 2 AB-Crystal 11.5mm x 5mm teardrop beads • 4 Rose 4mm faceted beads • 2 AB-Crystal 6mm faceted beads • 12" of Gold filled 24 gauge wire • 2 ear wires
INSTRUCTIONS: For each earring, cut 6" of wire. Make loop near one end of wire with round nose pliers. Slip teardrop on loop and wrap end of wire in a coil to secure, trim excess. Slip on beads as shown. Make loop in end. Attach to ear wire.

Rose & Crystal Bracelet

MATERIALS: 7 Rose 8mm faceted beads • 28 AB-Crystal 4mm faceted beads • 14 Rose 4mm faceted beads • 14 Gold filled 3mm beads • 24" of Clear elastic cord
INSTRUCTIONS: Cut two 12" lengths of cord. Both cords will go through some beads. If you have trouble getting both cords through a bead, slip first cord through bead, stretch cord by wrapping around forefinger and holding tight with thumb. The bead should be resting on top of forefinger. Slip second cord through hole. This will keep second cord from rubbing against first cord. Follow diagram below.

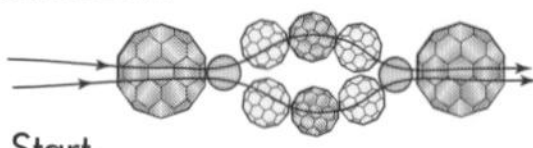

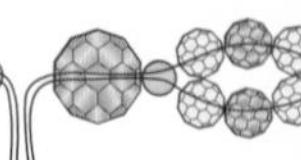

Crystal Bicone Bracelet

MATERIALS: 9 Gold filled 6mm beads • 36 Gold filled 3mm beads • 36 AB-Crystal 4mm bicone beads • 24" of Clear elastic cord
See instructions for Rose & Crystal Bracelet and use diagram below.

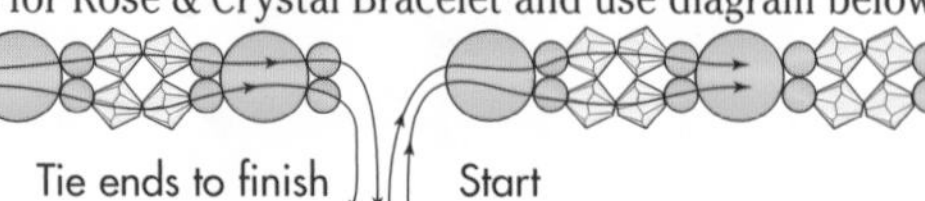

Crystal Bicone Earrings

MATERIALS: 2 Gold filled 6mm beads • 4 Gold filled 3mm beads • 2 AB-Crystal 8mm bicones • 4 Gold filled 1" head pins • 2 Gold filled ear posts with loop • 2 earring clutches
INSTRUCTIONS: For each earring, slip a 6mm bicone bead on head pin. Trim pin 1/4" above bead and make loop. Trim head off another pin, make a loop in same end and attach to bicone bead pin. Slip beads on pin as shown, make loop in end and attach to ear post.

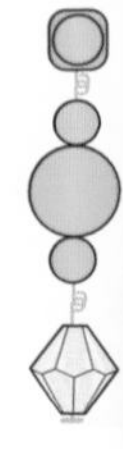

499 | 9781574211955 | 499

Location: BD-9

ZBM.136ST

: Crystals with Stretchy Cord (Design Originals) How to Make Jewelry using Clear Elastic Cord, including Lariat Necklaces, Bracelets, Pins, Earrings, Brooches, and Bags, Decorated with Ribbon and Beads

d: Very Good

e: 2023-10-30 12:40:41 (UTC)

KU: ZBM.136ST

_id: 12243762

rce: GRISELDA

delist unit# 12243762

XXXXX

heer color Necklaces

BY JANIE RAY

Amethyst, Aqua and Peridot are the stars here. Strung on clear elastic cord, these shimmery Crystal necklaces create an illusion of extravagant elegance with style.

Blue Illusion Necklace

MATERIALS: 9 Aqua 4mm faceted beads • 24" of Clear elastic cord • 2 Silver crimp beads • Silver barrel clasp with loops

INSTRUCTIONS: Center first bead on cord and add remaining Aqua beads following diagrams. Slip cord ends through loops on clasp, back through crimp beads and flatten crimps. Trim ends of cord.

Blue Illusion Beading Diagrams

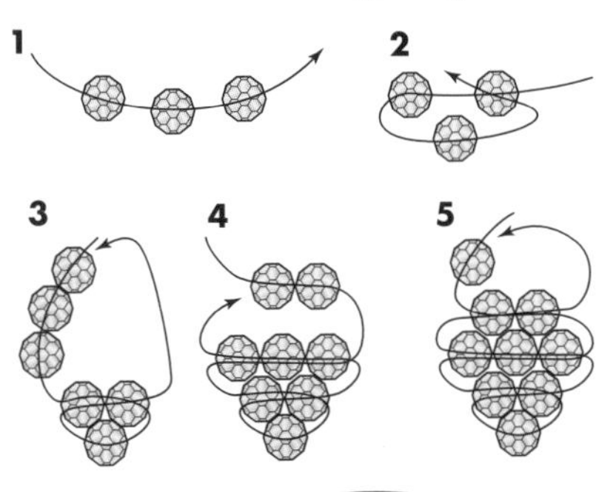

Amethyst Illusion Necklace

MATERIALS: 6 Light Amethyst 4mm faceted beads • Light Amethyst 6mm faceted bead • 20" of Clear elastic cord • 2 Silver crimp beads • Silver barrel clasp with loops

INSTRUCTIONS: Center first bead on cord and add remaining Amethyst beads following diagrams. Slip cord ends through loops on clasp, back through crimp beads and flatten crimps. Trim the ends of cord.

Amethyst Illusion Beading Diagrams

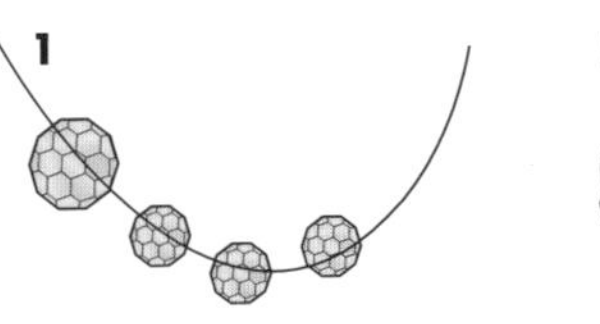

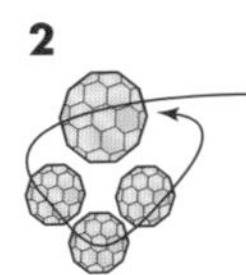

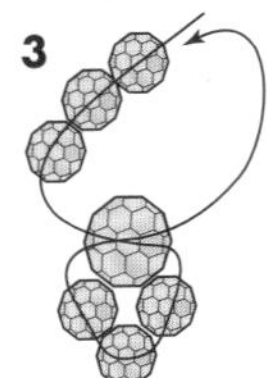

Peridot Illusion Necklace

MATERIALS: 10 Peridot 4mm faceted beads • 24" of Clear elastic cord • 2 Silver crimp beads • Silver barrel clasp with loops

INSTRUCTIONS: Center first bead on cord and add remaining Peridot beads following diagrams. Slip cord ends through loops on clasp, back through crimp beads and flatten crimps. Trim ends of the cord.

Peridot Illusion Beading Diagrams

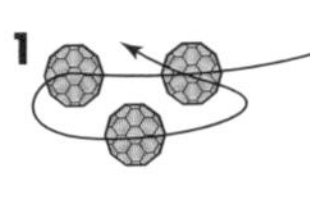

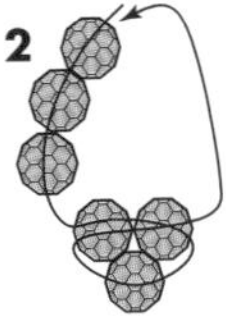

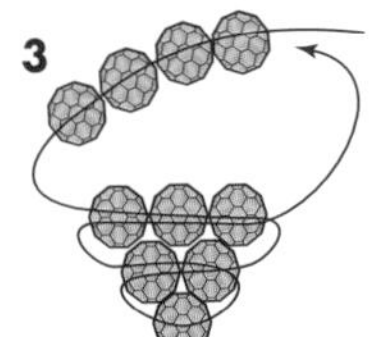

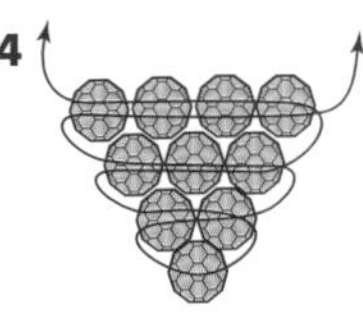

butterflies with Ribbon & Crystals

BY JANIE RAY

Pair lush greens with sheer purple, glimmery gold with brilliant topaz and vibrant sapphires with iridescent blue for sensational butterfly pins. You'll love how these bold and flirty accessories will dress up your wardrobe. They are fabulous for giving too!

Large Purple Butterfly
MATERIALS: 8mm, two 6mm and three 4mm AB-Crystal faceted beads • 9" and 6" lengths of 2" sheer Purple wire edge ribbon • 12" of Silver 24 gauge wire • Pin back • Needle and thread

Small Purple Butterfly
MATERIALS: 2 Sapphire 6mm faceted beads • 5 Sapphire 4mm faceted beads • 20 Iridescent Blue seed beads • 6" and 5" lengths of 7/8" Variegated Purple wire edge ribbon • 12" of Silver 24 gauge wire • Pin back • Needle and thread

Yellow Butterfly
MATERIALS: 8mm, 6mm and two 4mm Topaz faceted beads • 12 Iridescent 3mm beads • 5 1/2" and two 7 1/2" lengths of 1" sheer Yellow wire edge ribbon • 12" of Gold 24 gauge wire • Pin back • Needle and thread

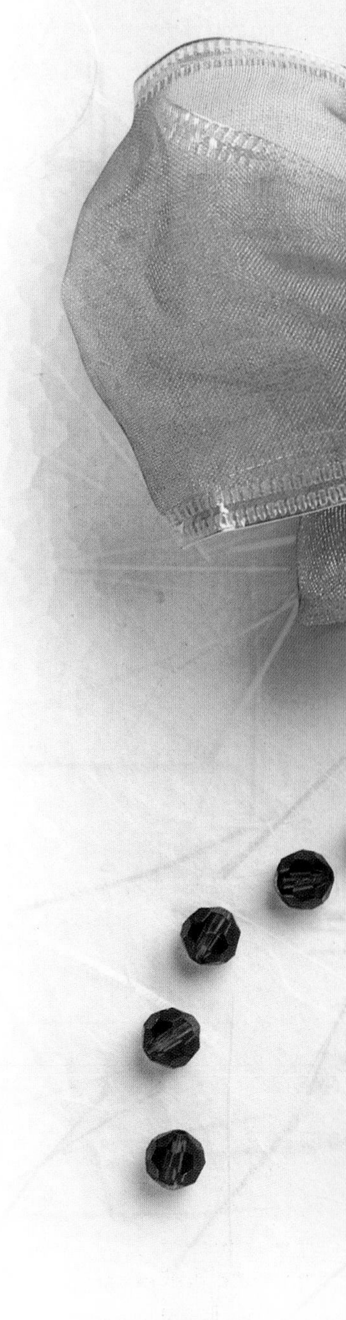

Ribbon & Crystal Pins

You'll find these wonderfully romantic pins and their instructions on pages 6 & 7.

1. Fold ribbon overl ping ends slightly. Tw wire around center wings. Do not cut wire.

Twist wire ends around
om wings.

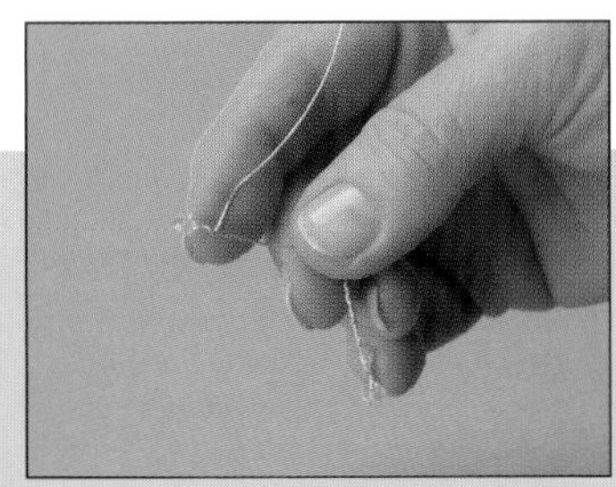

3. Thread beads on wire for antennae, twist together.

4. Add beads for body. Make loop in end to secure.

5. Secure body to wings with wire from wings. Sew pin on back.

Ribbons & Crystals

BY JANIE RAY

Brocade ribbon and crystals come together to create this back to the future jewelry. If you are looking for a quick and easy project this one is for you. Make a couple for your friends too!

1. Fold ends down diagonally and sew in place.

2. Fold end down and sew.

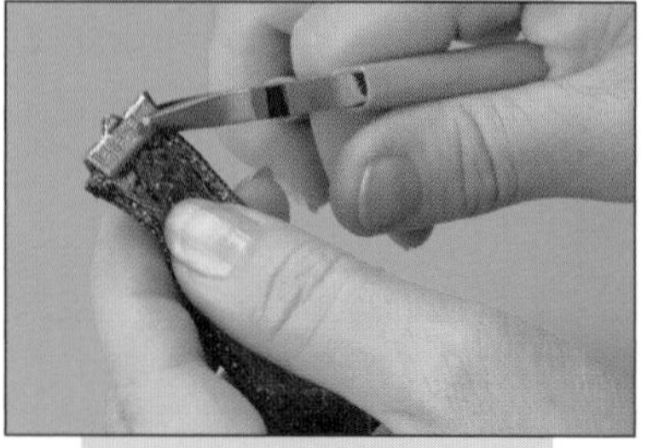

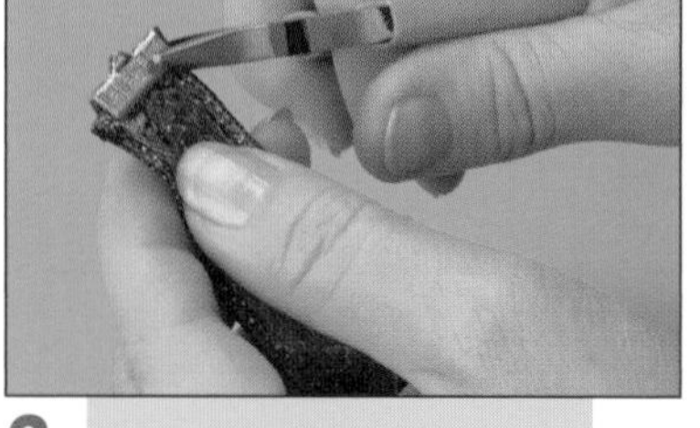

3. Attach ribbon clamp with flat nose pliers

Flower Ribbon Bracelet

MATERIALS: 8 Amethyst 4mm faceted beads • 4 Amethyst 6mm faceted beads • 2 Amethyst 8mm faceted beads • 14 Purple seed beads • 9" of ½" flower ribbon • Needle and Black thread • Snap

INSTRUCTIONS:

Fold each end of ribbon under ¼" and then ½", sew in place. Sew snap pieces on ends. Sew beads on ribbon as shown in photo.

Gold Ribbon Choker

MATERIALS: 5 Topaz 8mm faceted beads • 3 Topaz 6mm faceted beads • 4mm Topaz faceted bead • Gold seed beads • 2 Gold ribbon clamps • Gold hook • 16" of ⅞" Gold brocade ribbon • Beading thread and needle

INSTRUCTIONS:

Prepare ribbon referring to the photos 1 through 3. Sew the beaded dangles to the center of the ribbon as shown. Attach hook to clamp.

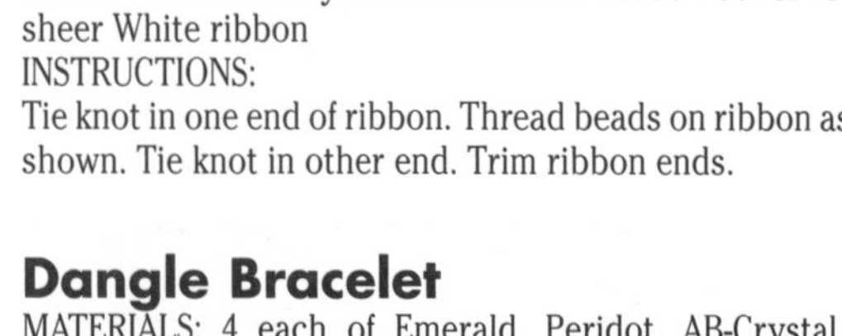

Crystal Ribbon Necklace

MATERIALS: 8 AB-Crystal 8mm faceted beads • 36" of ⅜" sheer White ribbon

INSTRUCTIONS:

Tie knot in one end of ribbon. Thread beads on ribbon as shown. Tie knot in other end. Trim ribbon ends.

Dangle Bracelet

MATERIALS: 4 each of Emerald, Peridot, AB-Crystal, Light Rose and Rose 8mm faceted beads • 4 each of Emerald, Peridot, AB-Crystal, Light Rose and Rose 6mm faceted beads • 6 each of Emerald, Peridot, AB-Crystal, Light Rose and Rose 4mm faceted beads • 10½" of 1¼" brocade ribbon • Beading thread and needle • Hook and loop dot

INSTRUCTIONS:

Fold each end of ribbon under ½" and then 1", sew in place. Sew dot pieces on ends. Make bead dangles and sew in place as shown.

fun & festive

Amulet Bags

BY JANIE RAY

1. Join ribbons for bag body with double sided adhesive.

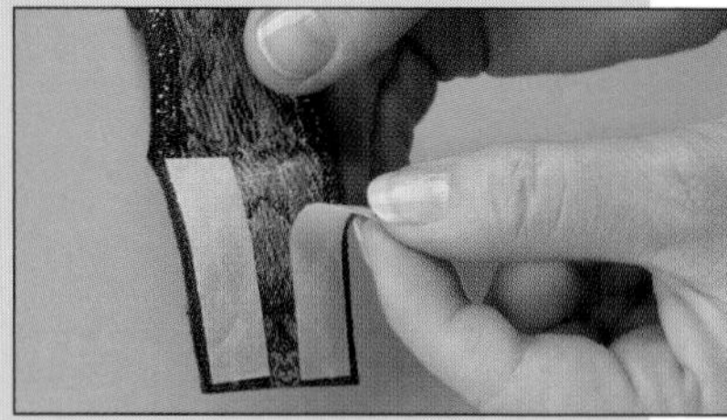

2. Press the adhesive on the decorative ribbon.

3. Fuse the hem in one end of the bag body.

4. Fuse the decorative ribbon to the bag body.

5. Fuse the hem in other end of bag body.

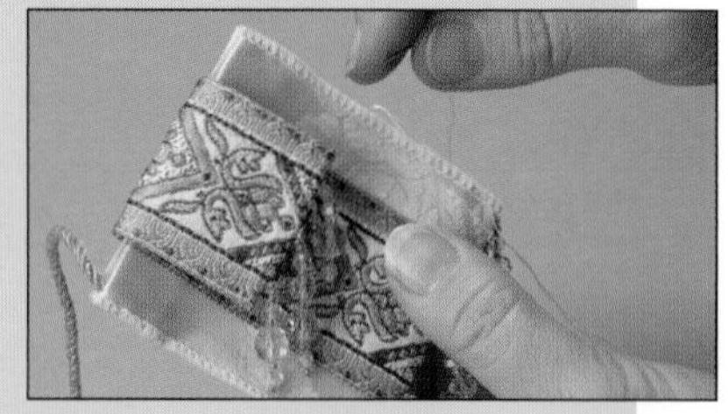

6. Sew sides of bag together adding braid for strap.

1. Fuse the ribbon to lining.

2. Fuse the hems in ends of bag.

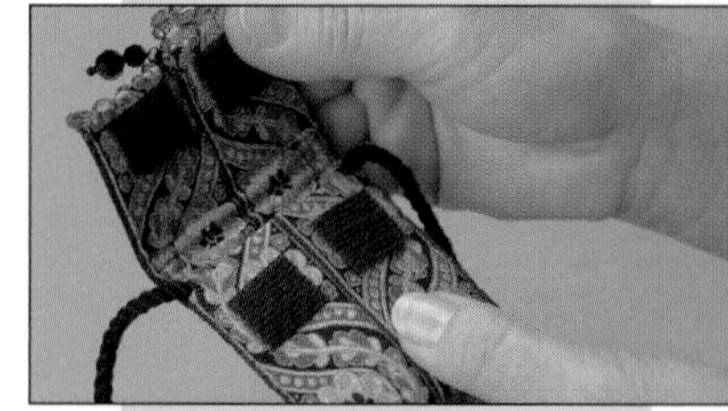

3. Attach hook and loop tape for the closure.

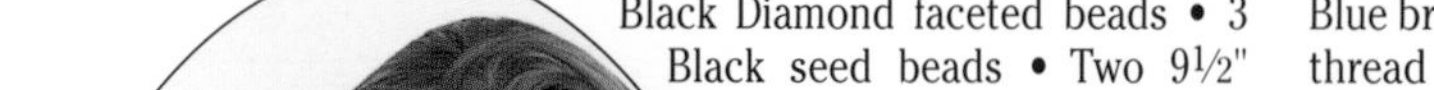

Black & Pink Purse

MATERIALS: Three each of 8mm, 6mm and 4mm Jet faceted beads • Three 8mm, six 6mm and twelve 4mm Black Diamond faceted beads • 3 Black seed beads • Two 9½" lengths of 1¼" brocade ribbon • 4" x 9½" piece of fabric for lining • 26" of Black cord • Needle and thread • Double sided fusing tape • Hook and loop dot or snap for closure

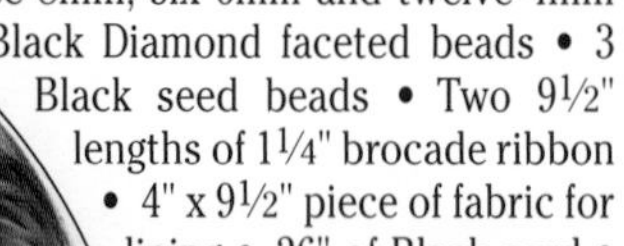

INSTRUCTIONS:

1. Fuse hems in sides of lining material. Fuse ribbons to wrong side of lining material. Turn under and fuse ½" hems in both ends of purse.
2. Fold purse and mark bottom line. Add bead dangles to bottom and flap edges referring to photo.
3. Sew the sides of purse catching the handle in stitching. Sew on a snap or dot for closure.

Blue Purse

MATERIALS: One 8mm, six 6mm and eight 4mm Sapphire faceted beads • 15 Gold 2mm beads • Two 8" lengths of 1½" Blue grosgrain ribbon • 11" of 1½" Blue brocade ribbon • 26" of Gold cord • Double sided fusing tape • Needle and thread • Hook and loop dot or snap for closure

INSTRUCTIONS:

1. Overlap ½" and fuse long edges of Blue grosgrain ribbons together. Fuse ½" hem in one end. Fold and fuse again. Fuse 2" hem in one end of Blue brocade ribbon. Fold corners of hemmed end into point and sew in place.
2. Fuse ribbon to purse body extending flap 1½" beyond hem. Fuse hem in other end of purse.
3. Sew sides of purse together catching handle in stitching.
4. Add bead dangles referring to photo. Sew on snap or dot for closure.

Cream & Pink Purse

MATERIALS: Six 8mm, four 6mm and eight 4mm Light Rose faceted beads • 8 AB-Crystal 4mm faceted beads • 50 Pink lined seed beads • 8" of 2½" Cream wire edge ribbon • 11" of 1½" Pink brocade ribbon • 26" of Gold and Pink cord • Needle and thread • Double sided fusing tape • Hook and loop dot or snap for closure

INSTRUCTIONS:

1. Fuse ½" hem in one end of Cream ribbon. Fold and fuse again. Fuse 2" hem in one end of Pink ribbon for flap.
2. Fuse the ribbon to the purse body extending flap 1½" beyond the hem. Fuse the hem in the other end of purse.
3. Fold in half and mark bottom line. Add bead dangles to bottom and flap edges referring to photo for bead placement.
4. Sew sides of purse catching handle in stitching. Sew on snap or dot for closure

exclusively yours

Fabulous Flutterbys

BY DEBORAH CAMPBELL

Poinsettia

MATERIALS: 21 Gold filled 3mm beads • 30 Siam 4mm bicone beads • 18" of Gold filled 24 gauge wire • Stick pin with pad

INSTRUCTIONS: Slip Gold, 6 Siam and Gold beads on wire. Twist to form loop leaving a 2" tail. Repeat to make 5 loops. Slip 11 Gold beads on 2" tail. Trim end of wire so that it is just long enough to bend over last bead and hold it in place. Use a drop of glue to secure last bead. Trim other wire. Glue flower on pad.

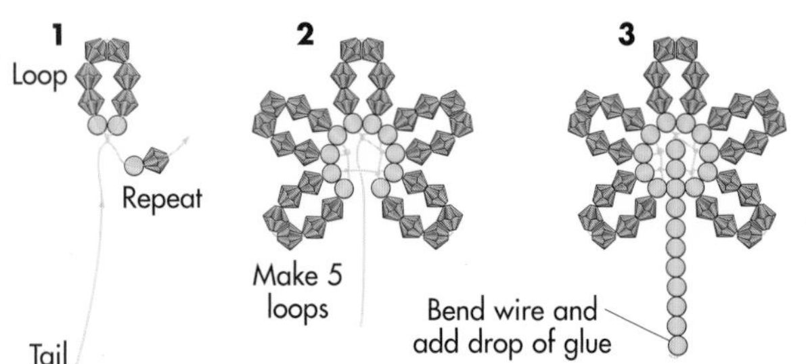

Tiny Angel

MATERIALS: 6mm AB-Crystal faceted bead • 6mm Crystal spacer bead • 9mm x 6mm Crystal teardrop • Gold stick pin with loop • 1½" Gold filled head pin • 6" of Gold filled 24 gauge wire

INSTRUCTIONS: Slip beads on a 1½" head pin. Make loop for halo on end of pin with round nose pliers. To make the wings, wrap wire around head pin above spacer bead. Make small loop on each side of wire. Twist loops to hold in place. Make 2 more loops. To flatten loops, squeeze with needle nose pliers. Make small loop to hang angel by wrapping one of the wires around round nose pliers and then around the other wire, trim excess wire. Attach angel to stick pin.

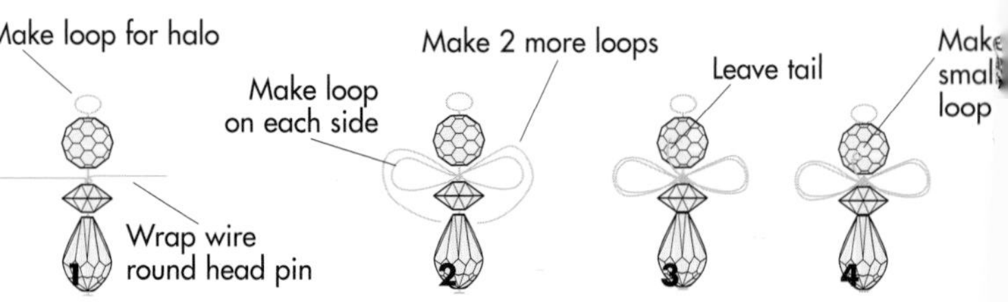